EL RAYADO

The Secrets of Congo Initiations

PALO MAYOMBE - PALO MONTE - KIMBISA

AMERICAN CANDOMBLE CHURCH PUBLICATIONS, LOS ANGELES

EL RAYADO

The Secrets of Congo Initiations

PALO MAYOMBE - PALO MONTE - KIMBISA

AMERICAN CANDOMBLE CHURCH
P.O. BOX 881377
LOS ANGELES, CALIFORNIA 90009

LEGAL DISCLAIMER

No part of this book may be reproduced in any manner without written permission from the publisher or the author of this book. This book contains formulas that were used in the historical AFRO-CARIBBEAN religious practices of Santeria, Palo Mayombe, Palo Monte and Kimbisa. The author and the publisher do not encourage any of the practices in this book nor do we assume any liabilities for presenting those formulas in this book. The formulas are presented for curious only. Neither the author nor the publisher, American Candomble Church assumes any responsibilities for the outcome of any of the spells, rituals or initiations in this book. We make no claims to any supernatural powers of these traditional initiation rituals. All inquiries or comments may be directed to the publisher. Warning: please be advised that all of the human bones and many of the animals used in these traditional magic formulas are available through biological supply distributors, taxidermy stores, zoos and museum stores. All of these items are available for sale on ebay. Grave digging, grave robbing and the use of endangered animals is illegal. Individuals must check with their individual state agencies and federal regulations to see if laws prohibit animal sacrifice, buying or selling of Human Bones and endangered animals. To investigate the legalities of animal sacrifice please refer to the Legal Case of *"Hialeah vs. The Church of Lucumi"* which established Santeria as a legitimate religion in the United States of America. You must be at least 18 years of age or older to purchase this book or to purchase any of the supplies listed herein.

TABLE OF CONTENTS

INTRODUCTION TO CONGO RITUALS

The "*Rayado Initiation Ceremony*" links the new initiate to the World of the Congo Spirits so that they will be better able to assist one with advancing in a positive direction in life. There are two parts of the *Rayado Initiation Ceremony*.

The first "*Rayado Initiation Ceremony*" establishes a spiritual relationship between the Congo Spirits and the new initiate.

The second "*Rayado Initiation Ceremony*," which is traditionally done 21 days after the first *Rayado Initiation Ceremony* gives the individual the ability to communicate and have command over the powerful Congo Deities.

Both *Rayado Initiation Ceremonies* give an individual great protection against all harmful energy that may be affecting the individual or that may come their way. The *Rayado Initiation Ceremony* gives the individual the ability to leap over all obstacles of this life and will even protect an individual from untimely death.

The *Rayado Initiation Ceremony* will make an individual invisible to any and all legal problems. This ceremony opens the third eye of the individual. It is only after doing these very important initiation ceremonies that an individual is fully accepted into the traditional Congo Munanzo Temple as a full-fledged member.

The *Rayado Initiation Ceremony* can save your life.

LAS REGLAS DE CONGO

The various Bantu (Congo) faiths in Cuba developed a particular religious tradition called with the general name of Palo. Palo in *Spanish* means "stick", due to the fact that sticks, roots etc. are used in this magical practice.

Since the beginning of the Trans-Atlantic Slave Trade when the Africans were brought to work as slaves on the sugar cane and coffee plantations there have existed various branches of the Congo religious tradition.

The various branches of the Bantu Cults are called "Reglas de Congo or Reglas de Palo" (Rules of Congo or Rules of Palo). There are many differences between those Traditions.

There are three main Congo religious trunks that exist in Cuba: ***Palo Mayombe***, ***Palo Brillumba*** and ***Palo Kimbisa***.

PALO MAYOMBE or MAYOMBE RULE

This is almost the first Congo Rule established in Cuba. They have only one kind of "fundamento nganga": Nsasi Siete Rayos. They deal only with nfumbe (deads) energies and are very traditional and conservative. The Batalla Saca Empenho, Mayombe Saca Mpenho, Ensala Mayombe Ngando Sese, Ensala Mayombe Ngando Batalla Congo are among the most famous "Ramas", branches of this Rule of Palo. Usually the Mayombe houses are not Christianized.

PALO BRILLUMBA or BRILLUMBA RULE

The religious tradition of Palo Brillumba is actually the most common. It's born from the Mayombe Rule. This Rule is syncretic and Christianized. They have various kinds of "fundamentos" like Siete Rayos, Zarabanda, Madre de Agua etc. Their Ngangas contain nfumbes and Mpungu (Kongo Gods) energies. The Mpungus can be considered in a way Congo versions of the Orixas. The Mpungus are also syncretized with Roman Catholic Saints. The term Brillumba is derived from the Congolese word "krillumba" that means "skull". The Brillumba Rule uses various types of bones including human in preparing their fundamentos. Many Paleros believe that more than a "Regla" itself, Brillumba, is a technique, a manner to prepare ngangas. There's also another type of Billumba Rule, they are Ndoki and non-Christianized. In this particular path of Brillumba, they also use bones in the preparation of the nganga. Brillumba is for good and evil purposes so it's called "Briyumba Ndoki Biyaya Biyaya Sambi". The Myth says that Brillumba was born in "Kunancieto" which means Africa. The territory was called "Consecration" in the Northern Kongo Kingdom. This is the history of "Briyumba.

PALO KIMBISA or KIMBISA RULE

The Kimbisa Rule was almost the first to be established in Cuba by the Kongo slaves. The Kimbisa were the High Priest of the Kingdom of Kongo. Many things inside this Rule show the evidence of its great antiquity, probably a direct descendant of the Kimpasi Secret Societies of Africa. The original Kimbisa Rule was not Christianized. During the XIX Century in the two Cabildos of the Church of the Saint Christ of the Good Journey in La Havana; the Rule of the Kimbisa Order as Saint Christ of the Good Journey was developed by *Tata Andrés Facundo Cristo de los Dolores Petit*, Founder of the Rule and great re-organizer of the Kimbisa Order. The Kimbisa Order has elements of ALL the various faiths and religions of the Cuban soil. Santo Cristo Buen Viaje is the first and totally Cuban Religion: Palo Monte Mayombe, Abakua, Santeria, Freemasonry, Espiritismo, Voudou, Roman Catholic Church are all parts of this Order.

RELIGIOUS HIERARCHY OF REGLA DE CONGO

All of the religious lines of the Regla De Congo follow a religious hierarchical structure which allows its initiates to achieve rank through various steps or degrees of initiations. The following is a list of various degrees in the Congo religious tradition.

FIRST DEGREE - NGUEYO

When an initiate receives their first rayado initiation they are refered to as *Ngueyo*. The word *Ngueyo* means to “start” or to “embark” on a journey. The new initiate is also refered to as *Pino Nuevo*, *Guatoko* or *Muchacho de Prenda*.

SECOND DEGREE - TATA NKISI

When an initiate receives their second rayado initiation they are refered to as *Tata Nkisi* (Men) or *Yaya Nkisi* (Women). Both the *Tata Nkisi* and the *Yaya Nkisi* begin to spiritually grow with the help of the Congo spirits, but within certain limits because they are not in possession of this religion's most central and sacred Item, the Nganga.

THIRD DEGREE - TATA NGANGA

The word *Tata Nganga* (Padre Nganga) or *Yaya Nganga* (Madre Nganga) refers to an initiate of the Congo religious tradition that has received their own personal Nganga or Fundamento to work with. A *Tata Nganga* is considered a priest of full religious degree because they have the right to conduct all of the sacred ceremonies and rituals of the Congo religious faith. A *Tata Nganga* who possesses their own spirit Nganga may form their own Munanzo or Congo religious temple. Often the term *Tata Nkisi* is considerate equal to *Padre Nganga* because in many cases the new Tata receives his Nganga at the same time, so actually the most important steps are those of *Ngueyo* and *Tata Nkisi*.

FOURTH DEGREE-TATA NDIBILONGO

When a *Tata Nganga* begins to have godchildren of their own and they start to initiate other individuals into the Congo religious tradition they are referred to as *Tata Ndibilongo*.

FIFTH DEGREE-TATA LUWONGO

Tata Luwongo or *Muluwanga Nkisi*, means Grandfather (abuelo de prenda) of the fundamento of the nganga. This is the highest degree of the Congo religious structure in the Palo Mayombe, Palo Monte and Kimbisa religious traditions.

THE RAYADO INITIATION CEREMONY

This book was written as a religious *"how to"* manual for initiated members of the Congo religious traditions of Palo Mayombe, Palo Monte and Kimbisa. At the writing of this book, I have had the opportunity to have had successfully initiated many individuals into the sacred Congo religious tradition and mysteries from all parts of the World. Although there may be some differences and variations of this particular initiation ceremony, the religious structure presented here of this complete religious ritual is the same as other Congo temples found throughout the World.

If your *Rayado Initiation Ceremony* was not done very similar to the following initiation ceremony presented here, then more than likely it was not done correctly and you should seek out an experienced Tata (Priest) from the Congo religion to correct it. The following Rayado Initiation Ceremony is how to do this very sacred ceremony in front of the *Congo Spirit Zarabanda.*

STEP I - THE CONGO DIVINATION CEREMONY

The interested individual (new initiate) must first consult with the Congo spirits with an experienced Tata (Congo Priest) using the *Chamalongo Divination System*. This can be done using the more commonly found and practiced simple (4) coconut shell *Chamalongo* method or it can be done using the full set of prepared *Chamalongo* (16) spirit seashells to determine if the individual will be allowed to enter into that particular Munanzo. If the spirits respond in favor of the individual, then the Tata will determine when the ceremony can take place and what the new individual must do before the actual *Rayado Initiation Ceremony* takes place.

STEP II - A SPIRITUAL OFFERING TO THE ANCESTORS

The individual must make a spiritual offering to their own ancestor spirits to receive permission to even proceed. This offering is usually placed on the floor directly in front of the *Eggun Spirits Ancestor Shrine* at the Congo Temple that you are seeking initiation into. When you bring the offering, the Tata will call upon the Ancestors from the temple and from your family to witness the sacred ceremony.

A SPIRITUAL FOOD OFFERING TO THE EGGUN SPIRITS

1. WHITE PLATE
2. ONE COCONUT
3. THREE HOUSEHOLD CANDLES (WHITE)
4. ONE GLASS OF FRESH WATER
5. ONE BOTTLE OF WHITE RUM (CACHACA/AGUARDIENTE)
6. THE SPIRITUAL OFFERING OF $21.00 (DERECHO)
7. A PACK OF TABACCO CIGARS

SOMETIMES THE ANCESTORS WILL REQUIRE A BLOOD OFFERING (EBO) SUCH AS A ROOSTER OR A HEN. THE SPIRITS MAY ALSO REQUIRE A COOKED HOT FOOD OFFERING (ADDIMU) SUCH AS RICE AND BEANS, YUCCA, POTATOES AND EVEN COOKED MEAT OR POULTRY. DURING YOUR INITIAL CONSULTATION WITH THE CHAMALONGO, THE TATA WILL DETERMINE WHAT THE ANCESTOR SPIRITS REQUIRE IN ORDER TO PROCEED WITH THE RAYADO INITIATION CEREMONY. THIS CEREMONY MUST BE DONE IN ORDER TO ENSURE THE SUCCESS OF THE RAYADO INITIATION.

STEP III

After completing *STEP II,* the individual can proceed to STEP III. I also would like to add the comment that the (new initiate) must complete the Rayado ritual within 21 days if the individual will not be receiving their Rayado initiation the same day as presenting the offering to the Eggun Spirits. If the individual waits more than 21 days from the time that they present the offerings to the Eggun Spirits, there may be a change in the individual's spiritual destiny as foretold by the Chamalongos and they will have to have the Tata read the Chamalongos once again to determine if the spiritual alignment of the individual has not changed since the last Chamalongo divination reading.

When the individual arrives at the Munanzo for the initiation ritual, they must bring all of the following items:

A COMPLETE CHANGE OF "NEW" WHITE CLOTHES
A WHITE BANDANA
A WHITE PLATE
ONE COCONUT
(3) HOUSEHOLD CANDLES (WHITE)
ONE LARGE BOTTLE OF WHITE RUM (CACHACA/AGUARDIENTE)
ONE PACKAGE OF TABACCO CIGARS
ONE "NEW" WHITE TOWEL
BLACK ROOSTERS (2)
THE SPIRITUAL OFFERING (DERECHO)

STEP IV - THE ROMPEMIENTO (SPIRITUAL CLEANSING)

The spiritual purification ritual that the individual will first have done by the Tata or by the other members of the Congo temple is called "*rompemiento*". The *rompemiento* ceremony is a spiritual cleansing done using cigar smoke, rum, black soap and omiero herbal bath liquid. The cleansing is done by the priests present praying over the individual who will become initiated by reciting a series of Congo prayers that are said to the spirits so they will spiritually descend upon the cleansing ceremony to free the individual from any type of negative vibration. The *rompemiento* ceremony is usually done outside in a special area of the Congo temple. When the prayers are finished, the individual will have their clothes cut and then ritually torn off their bodies and then bathed in a special herbal bath liquid mixture known as omiero. This omiero is a mixture of various herbs and is ritually prepared and magically charged for maximum strength and spiritual power. The tearing of the clothes represents the individual leaving their past life behind and to prepare for a brand new spiritual life. The individual should be given authentic real African Black Soap to use while they are bathing. The Congo temple is a sacred holy place of God and therefore all individuals that are allowed to participate in the Rayado Initiation Ceremony should also take an omiero spiritual bath at home before coming to the temple to assist in the ceremony. When coming to the Congo Munanzo to assist the Tata with the initiation process, you must learn to leave your problems outside and away from the temple. Remember, this is a very special day for the new initiate and your full attention, focus and spiritual concentration is necessary to ensure the spiritual success of the Congo *Rayado Initiation Ceremony.*

IF YOU ARE A PALERO PRIEST INITIATING A NEW FEMALE INITIATE, PLEASE STAY SPIRITUALLY FOCUSED AND AVOID ANY SEXUAL THOUGHTS WHILE DOING THE ROMPEMIENTO. SEXUAL MISCONDUCT AND IMMORALITY ARE STRICTLY PROHIBITED IN ALL CONGO TEMPLES IN THE "REGLA DE CONGO".

IF YOU THINK THAT YOU WILL HAVE A PROBLEM WITH THE "REGLA DE CONGO" HAVE SOMEONE WHO IS MORE EXPERIENCED DO THE CLEANSING CEREMONY.

RESPECT ALL INDIVIDUALS AT ALL TIMES.

STEP V

After the individual has finished bathing, they will be allowed to towel dry and instructed to put on their new white clothes. The new initiate will be then blind folded with the white bandana and led to the Congo Temple ritual initiation area and made to kneel down on a straw mat and then be placed in a position of facing the wall until the initiation begins. This process is called ***"penetencia"***. This is a time for the initiate to reflect on their past life and to think about what they are about to do. This is also the time for the initiate to start to focus on their ancestor spirits, their spirit guides and the Congo spirits and also for the spirits to start to surround the initiate to start bringing them blessings. The new initiate will remain kneeling until the initiation ceremony begins. This "*penetencia*" time usually last about 1 to 3 hours depending on your particular Congo temple.

ALL OF THE TORNED AND CUT CLOTHES OF THE INDIVIDUAL SHOULD BE PLACED INTO A LARGE CLOTH BURLAP BAG AND PLACED TO ONE SIDE OF THE TEMPLE AREA FOR NOW. THIS BAG ALONG WITH THE BODIES OF THE SACRIFICED ROOSTERS AND 21 PENNIES MUST BE TAKEN TO A RAILROAD CROSSING OR TO A CEMETERY AND LEFT THERE AT THE END OF THE RAYADO INITIATION CEREMONY BY THE NEW INITIATE.

STEP VI

When the time arrives for the Rayado initiation to begin, the initiate will be led to the initiation area where the primary spiritual nganga resides and where the Rayado ceremony will take place. The initiate will be led outside so that the initiate will re-enter the *"CUARTO DE MUERTO"* the spirit room in the appropriate formal manner. The new initiate will follow blindly a member from the Congo temple into the ritual area by placing their right hand on the left shoulder of the temple member. The new initiate will be instructed to knock on the temple door "(3) times" and the Congo Temple member who is assisting the new initiate will tell him or her what to say. When the new initiate knocks (3) times on the temple door, the Tata from behind the door will respond by saying the following:

(TATA): Who knocks on this sacred Congo Temple door?

(NEW INITIATE): The individual will state their full birth name.

(TATA): The Tata will then say the following; What do you seek here?

(NEW INITIATE): The new initiate responds saying the following; I seek new life, I seek the spirit (the name of the spirit nagnga that the individual will receive their Rayado on) and I seek all of the good things in this life. After saying this, the Tata will say the following:

(TATA): "*Cuenda*" or ENTER.

Following the temple member, the initiate will be led directly in front of the nganga and again be asked to kneel down. The member who led the new initiate to the initiation area will then stand behind the new initiate with their right hand on the right shoulder of the new initiate. The member will be holding a white candle that is lit in the other hand. The initiate will then be presented to hold the white plate which will contain all of the offerings on it that they brought to the temple.

A WHITE PLATE, ONE COCONUT, (3) HOUSEHOLD CANDLES (WHITE), ONE LARGE BOTTLE OF WHITE RUM (CACHACA/AGUARDIENTE), ONE PACKAGE OF TABACCO CIGARS, ONE "NEW" WHITE TOWEL, BLACK ROOSTERS (2), THE SPIRITUAL OFFERING (DERECHO)

(TATA): The priest will then ask the initiate the following question: (name of the new initiate) Do you swear on your blood to never reveal to anybody what you will go through and see tonight?

(NEW INITIATE): The new initiate responds: I swear on my life and on my blood.

(TATA): The priest then asks again to the "new initiate", What do you seek?

(NEW INITIATE): The new initiate responds: I have come here seeking a new life and I seek the Mysteries and the secrets of Congo Spirits and of this Congo Munanzo (the name of the particular Munanzo).

STEP VII

The members of the temple will then begin singing traditional Congo religion Mambos.

(THE CONGO MAMBOS ARE SUNG REPEATEDLY UNTIL YOU BEGIN TO FEEL THE ENERGY OF THE SPIRITS TO START TO DESCEND UPON THE CEREMONY)

After singing the Congo Mambos then proceed to **STEP VIII**.

STEP VIII

The Tata standing in front of the new initiate and the other members of the Congo temple standing behind the individual (new initiate) The Tata will begin reciting the following prayers and the other members responding to the following prayers. While the Tata is reciting the prayers, the Bakunfula who is the right hand of the Tata and the regulator of the temple and all its religious functions starts tapping in sync directly in front of the Congo Spirits Nganga with the Congo prayers the *"Baston De Muerto"*.

(TATA): *CON LA LICENCIA DE NZAMBI*

(MEMBERS): *SALA MALEKUN, MALEKUN SALA*

(TATA): *CON LA LICENCIA DE EGGUN QUE ESTAN EN LOS PIES DE NZAMBI*

(MEMBERS): *SALA MALEKUN, MALEKUN SALA*

(TATA): *CON LA LICENCIA DE EXU (LUCERO)*

(MEMBERS): *SALA MALEKUN, MALEKUN SALA*

(TATA): *CON LA LICENCIA DE LUKANKANSE*

(MEMBERS): *SALA MALEKUN, MALEKUN SALA*

(TATA): *CON LA LICENCIA DE KOBAYENDE*

(MEMBERS): *SALA MALEKUN, MALEKUN SALA*

(TATA): *CON LA LICENCIA DE CENTELLE NDOKI*

(MEMBERS): *SALA MALEKUN, MALEKUN SALA*

(TATA): *CON LA LICENCIA DE GURUNFINDA*

(MEMBERS): *SALA MALEKUN, MALEKUN SALA*

(TATA): *CON LA LICENCIA DE MADRE DE AGUA*

(MEMBERS): *SALA MALEKUN, MALEKUN SALA*

(TATA): *CON LA LICENCIA DE MAMA CHOLA*

(MEMBERS): *SALA MALEKUN, MALEKUN SALA*

(TATA): *CON LA LICENCIA DE TIEMPO VIEJO*

(MEMBERS): *SALA MALEKUN, MALEKUN SALA*

(TATA): *CON LA LICENCIA DE CABO RONDO*

(MEMBERS): *SALA MALEKUN, MALEKUN SALA*

(TATA): *CON LA LICENCIA DE SIETE RAYOS*

(MEMBERS): *SALA MALEKUN, MALEKUN SALA*

(TATA): *CON LA LICENCIA DE NSAMBA NTALA*

(MEMBERS): *SALA MALEKUN, MALEKUN SALA*

(TATA): *SOMOS O NO SOMOS*

(MEMBERS): *SOMOS*

(TATA): *SOMOS O NO SOMOS*

(MEMBERS): *SOMOS*

(TATA): *SOMOS O NO SOMOS*

(MEMBERS): *SOMOS*

(TATA): OJO POR OJO
DIENTE POR DIENTE
PERRO NO COME PERRO
LA MATRACA MATA SU MADRE
SOMOS O NO SOMOS
SOMOS O NO SOMOS
SOMOS O NO SOMOS
ZARABANDA BRILLUMBI NDOKI INFIERNO VIRA MUNDO
ZARABANDA BRILLUMBI NDOKI INFIERNO VIRA MUNDO
ZARABANDA BRILLUMBI NDOKI INFIERNO VIRA MUNDO
ZARABANDA BRILLUMBI NDOKI INFIERNO VIRA MUNDO
ZARABANDA BRILLUMBI NDOKI INFIERNO VIRA MUNDO
ZARABANDA BRILLUMBI NDOKI INFIERNO VIRA MUNDO
ZARABANDA BRILLUMBI NDOKI INFIERNO VIRA MUNDO
ZARABANDA BRILLUMBI NDOKI INFIERNO VIRA MUNDO
ZARABANDA BRILLUMBI NDOKI INFIERNO VIRA MUNDO
WHO IS THE GREATEST IN HEAVEN? NZAMBI
WHO IS THE GREATEST IN HEAVEN? NZAMBI
WHO IS THE GREATEST IN HEAVEN? NZAMBI
WHO ARE YOU? ZARABANDA
WHO ARE YOU? ZARABANDA
WHO ARE YOU? ZARABANDA

AFTER SAYING THIS PRAYER THE CEREMONY PROCEEDS WITH THE TATA SAYING THE FOLLOWING WORDS AND BY THEN ASKING THE NEW INITIATE THE FOLLOWING QUESTIONS:

(TATA): *You are here in this sacred temple and this sacred place.*

1. *Do you still wish to continue with this ceremony?*

2. *Do you swear on your blood to never reveal anything about this ceremony to anyone?* - If the new initiate replies yes then the initiation ritual continues -

STEP IX

AFTER THE MEMBERS HAVE FINISHED RECITING THE PRAYERS, EACH MEMBER WILL COME UP TO THE NGANGA AND USING PEMBA/TIZO *"WHITE CHALK"* WILL EACH DRAW OUT ON THE FLOOR DIRECTLY IN FRONT OF THE NGANGA THE CONGO SPIRIT SIGNATURE (FIRMA) THAT EACH OF THEM RECEIVED AFTER THEIR SECOND RAYADO CEREMONY. THE FIRMA OR THE SACRED SPIRITUAL SIGNATURE (SPIRIT SIGIL) IS UNIQUE TO EACH PARTICULAR MUNANZO MEMBER. IT IS ONLY BY DRAWING THIS SECRET FIRMA ON THE FLOOR DIRECTLY IN FRONT OF THE NGANGA THAT THE CONGO SPIRITS WILL RECOGNIZE THE SECRET SPIRITUAL IDENTITY OF EACH MEMBER WHO IS PRESENT AT THE INITIATION CEREMONY. AFTER THE CEREMONY IS COMPLETEY FINISHED, THESE SECRET FIRMAS WILL BE WASHED AWAY USING WHITE RUM OR CHAMBA.

STEP X

The Tata will take the bottle of Chamba and blow it directly over the nganga and the new initiate (3 times). After this, the Tata will then light a cigar and blow the smoke directly over the nganga and over the new initiate. After this, the Tata and the Bakunfula will ritually clean the new initiate with one of the live roosters and then sacrifice it over the nganga and allow the blood to pour into the Spirit Nganga allowing the *"Nkisi"* to feed and to gain power and strength before proceeding to the next step. After the rooster is sacrificed, it is placed into the burlap bag along with the initiates torn and cut clothes from the rompemiento cleansing ceremony.

STEP XI THE PRESENTATION

In the presentation ceremony, the individual is presented various sacred items of the Spirit Nganga and of Congo temple. The new initiate will once again swear on their blood with each of the items presented to them. Before the Tata and the Bakunfula present the sacred items the initiate will be asked the following questions and will swear on their blood to each of these questions.

(**TATA**): *(Say the name of the new initiate) - Do you swear on your life and on your blood to always respect your Godfather?*

(**NEW INITIATE**): *YES*

(**TATA**): *(Say the name of the new initiate) - Do you swear on your life and on your blood to be loyal and respect your Congo Munanzo?*

(**NEW INITIATE**): *YES*

(**TATA**): *(Say the name of the new initiate) - Do you swear on your life and on your blood to never reveal any of the sacred secret mysteries of this Congo Munanzo?*

(**NEW INITIATE**): *YES*

(**TATA**): *(Say the name of the new initiate) - Do you swear on your life and on your blood to be a good man?*

(**NEW INITIATE**): *YES*

(**TATA**): *(Say the name of the new initiate) - Do you swear on your life and on your blood to be a good and faithful Godson?*

(**NEW INITIATE**): *YES*

(**TATA**): *(Say the name of the new initiate) - Do you swear on your life and on your blood to be a good Congo Brother?*

(**NEW INITIATE**): *YES*

(**TATA**): *(Say the name of the new initiate) - Do you swear on your life and on your blood to be a good Husband to your Wife?*

(**NEW INITIATE**): *YES*

(TATA): *(Say the name of the new initiate) - Do you swear on your life and on your blood to be a good Father?*

(**NEW INITIATE**): *YES*

(**TATA**): *(Say name of the new initiate) - Do you swear on your life and on your blood to keep the secrets of this Congo Munanzo secretive and uphold its honor of our Congo tradition?*

(NEW INITIATE): *YES*

(TATA): *(Say the name of the new initiate) - Do you swear on your life and on your blood to defend this temple with your life?*

(**NEW INITIATE**): *YES*

(TATA): *(Say the name of the new initiate) - Do you swear on your life and on your blood that you will not regret what you are going to do at this initiation in the morning?*

(**NEW INITIATE**): *YES*

The Tata will then take the following items and present it to the individual in the following order: THE CONGO SPIRIT *LUCERO, A PALO "STICK", A PIECE OF TIZO (CHALK), THE CANA BRAVA, THE MPAKA FROM THE NGANGA SPIRIT* and lastly a *HUMAN TIBIA BONE FROM THE NGANGA SPIRIT.*

(The Tata Priest and the Bakunfula will present the sacred items directly on all of the areas and points where the new initiate will be "scratched" on).

As the Tata finishes presenting each of the sacred items the members will sing a mambo to each of the sacred ritual items.

1. Place the *"CONGO SPIRIT LUCERO"* into the hands of the new initiate who is kneeling down and still blind folded and say the following:

(TATA): *What do you have in your hands?*

(**NEW INITIATE**): The new initiate will then say: *I don't know.*

(TATA): *This is the Spirit Lucero, The Keeper of the Crossroads and the Divine Gate Keeper. It is through the Spirit Lucero that you were able to be here and present tonight. It is the Spirit Lucero who led you here to this Munanzo tonight. It is through the Spirit Lucero that your destiny begins and ends. It is through the Spirit Lucero that all magic begins and ends. It is through the Spirit Lucero that your new life begins here tonight at this temple at this very holy and sacred of all places. May the Spirit Lucero light your roads in darkness so that you will never lose your way home. May the Spirit Lucero guide and protect you so that you will always have a roof over your head. May the Spirit Lucero always have food on your table. May the Spirit Lucero always provide that you have money in your pockets. May the Spirit Lucero always give you good health. May the Spirit Lucero always give you victory over all of your enemies known and unknown. May the Spirit Lucero banish all tragedy in your path. May the Spirit Lucero never allow you to be arrested. May the Spirit Lucero never allow you to be placed behind bars. May the Spirit Lucero never allow you to be placed in front of a judge or a jury against you. May the Spirit Lucero give you the ability to always be able to leap over all obstacles in your life, like the deer that leaps over their obstacles.*

(TATA): Do you swear on your life and on your blood tonight to the Spirit Lucero?

(NEW INITIATE): Yes, I swear

(TATA): Tell the new initiate to kiss the Spirit Lucero, (3) times.

(TATA): Present the Spirit Lucero to the new initiates (forehead, both hands, both shoulders, the back of the neck and to both back of the legs) while singing the following Mambo song:

(TATA & TEMPLE MEMBERS): *Juran Lucero, Juran Lucero Yo, Juran Lucero, Juran Lucero Yo, Juran Lucero, Juran Lucero Yo, Juran Lucero, Juran Lucero Yo, Juran Lucero, Juran Lucero Yo, Juran Lucero, Juran Lucero Yo.*

2. Place the sacred "*PALO*" stick into the hands of the new initiate who is kneeling down and still blind folded and say the following:

(**TATA**): *What do you have in your hands?*

(**NEW INITIATE**): The new initiate will then say*: I don't know.*

(**TATA**): *This is the sacred "finda". Finda is herb in Congo. It is also called "palo". "Finda" was placed here on this earth by Nzambi (God) to heal and to make magic work. This sacred item has a spirit associated with it. The herbs are sacred to the Congo Spirits. All finda contains a unique power to its own. Each of the Spirits represented here tonight have their own unique "finda" that is sacred only to them. By invoking the magical powers of the finda, there is nothing that you can't do. This "finda" is round. It is round because it symbolizes that because it is round it can roll. Just as this "Finda", or "palo" can roll so shall you to by receiving this sacred ceremony be also able to roll over all of your enemies and obstacles in your life.*

(TATA): Do you swear on your life and on your blood tonight to this Palo and to this sacred Finda?

(NEW INITIATE): Yes, I swear

(TATA): Tell the new initiate to kiss the "PALO", (3) times.

(TATA): Present the "PALO" to the new initiates (forehead, both hands, both shoulders, the back of the neck and to both back of the legs) while singing the following Mambo song:

(TATA & TEMPLE MEMBERS): *Juran Palo, Juran Palo Yo, Juran Palo, Juran Palo Yo, Juran Finda, Juran Finda Yo, Juran Finda, Juran Finda Yo, Juran Palo, Juran Palo Yo, Juran Palo, Juran Palo Yo.*

3. Place the sacred "TIZO" (White Chalk/Pemba) into the hands of the new initiate who is kneeling down and still blind folded and say the following:

(TATA): *What do you have in your hands?*

(**NEW INITIATE**): The new initiate will then say*: I don't know.*

(TATA): *This is the sacred "tizo". Tizo is a powerful spirit. Tizo is sacred to the Congo Spirits because without it they can't write their names or know our names. Tizo is used to draw out the powerful spirit signatures which when drawn and then properly invoked bring forth magic and new life. The color of Tizo is white. White represents purity and light. White represents the bones of the Spirits that you are making a pact here tonight.*

(TATA): Do you swear on your life and on your blood tonight to the spirit of this Tizo?

(NEW INITIATE): Yes, I swear

(TATA): Tell the new initiate to kiss the "TIZO", (3) times.

(TATA): Present the "TIZO" to the new initiates (forehead, both hands, both shoulders, the back of the neck and to both back of the legs) while singing the following Mambo song:

(TATA & TEMPLE MEMBERS): *Juran Tizo, Juran Tizo Yo, Juran Tizo, Juran Tizo, Yo, Juran Tizo, Juran Tizo Yo, Juran Tizo, Juran Tizo Yo, Juran Tizo, Juran Tizo Yo, Juran Tizo, Juran Tizo Yo.*

4. Place the sacred "CANA BRAVA" into the hands of the new initiate who is kneeling down and still blind folded and say the following:

(TATA): *What do you have in your hands?*

(**NEW INITIATE**): The new initiate will then say: *I don't know.*

(TATA): *This is the sacred "CANA BRAVA". Cana Brava is a powerful spirit. Cana Brava is sacred to the Congo Spirits because it is the spiritual thermometer of the Nganga. Without it the Congo Spirits would be unbalanced just as you would be unbalanced without the Congo Spirits. Within the Cana Brava it contains all of the elements to cool down the Congo Spirits just as the Congo Spirits contain all of the elements that you will need in this life to remain cool and balanced.*

(TATA): Do you swear on your life and on your blood tonight to the spirit of this CANA BRAVA?

(NEW INITIATE): Yes, I swear

(TATA): Tell the new initiate to kiss the "CANA BRAVA", (3) times.

(TATA): Present the "CANA BRAVA" to the new initiates (forehead, both hands, both shoulders, the back of the neck and to both back of the legs) while singing the following Mambo song:

(TATA & TEMPLE MEMBERS): *Juran Cana Brava, Juran Cana Brava Yo, Juran Cana Brava, Juran Cana Brava Yo, Juran Cana Brava, Juran Cana Brava Yo, Juran Cana Brava, Juran Cana Brava Yo, Juran Cana Brava, Juran Cana Brava Yo, Juran Cana Brava, Juran Cana Brava Yo.*

5. Place the sacred "MPAKA" into the hands of the new initiate who is kneeling down and still blind folded and say the following:

(TATA): *What do you have in your hands?*

(**NEW INITIATE**): The new initiate will then say*: I don't know.*

(TATA): *This is the sacred "MPAKA". The Mpaka contains a powerful spirit. The Mpaka contains all of the spiritual elements which exist and found within nature to give the Spirits life. It is through the Mpaka that the Congo Spirits can be manifested within our World. It is through the Mpaka that the spirits can see, hear and smell you. The Mpaka It is also called "Vititi Mensu", the all-seeing spirit eye because it has a mirror as its eyes. Through the Vititi Mensu, the mirrored eye, the spirits can repeal all evil and banish all evil that our enemies may send our way. The sacred Mpaka contains all of sacred mysteries of our belief within it and therefore through the Mpaka the Spirits can be born and given new life just as you are being born here tonight into a new life. A new life protected by the all-powerful eye of the Vititi Mensu, Mpaka.*

(TATA): Do you swear on your life and on your blood tonight to the spirit of this MPAKA?

(NEW INITIATE): Yes, I swear

(TATA): Tell the new initiate to kiss the "MPAKA", (3) times.

(TATA): Present the "MPAKA" to the new initiates (forehead, both hands, both shoulders, the back of the neck and to both back of the legs) while singing the following Mambo song:

(TATA & TEMPLE MEMBERS): *Juran Mpaka, Juran Mpaka Yo, Juran Mpaka, Juran Mpaka Yo, Juran Mpaka, Juran*

Mpaka Yo, Juran Mpaka, Juran Mpaka Yo,Juran Mpaka, Juran Mpaka Yo.

6. Place the sacred "TIBIA" into the hands of the new initiate who is kneeling down and still blind folded and say the following:

(TATA): *What do you have in your hands?*

(**NEW INITIATE**): The new initiate will then say*: I don't know.*

(TATA): *This is the sacred "HUESO". HUESO is a powerful spirit. HUESO is sacred to the Congo Spirits because it represents strength, vitality and new life. Without the Hueso the spirits could not walk just as you would not be able to walk without the Congo Spirits. It is through Hueso that the Congo Spirits will protect you.*

(TATA): Do you swear on your life and on your blood tonight to the spirit of this HUESO?

(NEW INITIATE): Yes, I swear

(TATA): Tell the new initiate to kiss the "HUESO", (3) times and then bite down on it (3) times.

(TATA): Present the "HUESO" to the new initiates (forehead, both hands, both shoulders, the back of the neck and to both back of the legs) while singing the following Mambo song:

(TATA & TEMPLE MEMBERS) : *Juran Hueso, Juran Hueso Yo, Juran Hueso, Juran Hueso Yo, Juran Hueso, Juran Hueso Yo, Juran Hueso, Juran Hueso Yo, Juran Hueso, Juran Hueso Yo, Juran Hueso, Juran Hueso Yo.*

7. Place the sacred "MBELE" into the hands of the new initiate who is kneeling down and still blind folded and say the following:

(TATA): *What do you have in your hands?*

(**NEW INITIATE**): The new initiate will then say*: I don't know.*

(TATA): *This is the sacred "MBELE". The Mbele is a powerful spirit. The Mbele is the sacred Machete of the Congo Spirits. The Mbele represents law and order. The Mbele is used to punish the enemies of the Congo Spirits just as they will punish you if you ever disrespect them, disrespect your temple, disrespect your Tata or disrespect the other members of this temple. The Mbele is used to cut down all negative and unwanted things in the spirits path just as they will cut away and down all of your enemies and negative obstacles in your life.*

(TATA): Do you swear on your life and on your blood tonight to the spirit of this MBELE?

(NEW INITIATE): Yes, I swear

(TATA): Tell the new initiate to kiss the "MBELE", (3) times.

(TATA): Present the "MBELE" to the new initiates (forehead, both hands, both shoulders, the back of the neck and to both back of the legs) while singing the following Mambo song:

(TATA & TEMPLE MEMBERS) : *Juran Mbele, Juran Mbele Yo, Juran Mbele, Juran Mbele Yo, Juran Mbele, Juran Mbele Yo, Juran Mbele, Juran Mbele Yo, Juran Mbele, Juran Mbele Yo, Juran Mbele, Juran Mbele Yo.*

STEP XII

After the presentation ceremony, give the new initiate (3) YAMBUZO tablets to swallow one at at time in their mouth and a glass of omiero made from 21 herbs to drink to wash them down. After they swallow all (3) YAMBUZO tablets and drink all of the Omiero, then give the new initiate (3) capfuls of Chamba to drink.

IF THE NEW INITIATE HAS BEEN THE VICTIM OF ANY WITCHCRAFT ATTACKS IN THE PAST THE INDIVIDUAL WILL AUTOMATICALLY START TO VOMIT IT UP SO PLEASE HAVE A PLASTIC BAG PRESENT TO PLACE IT IN. IF THE INDIVIDUAL VOMITS UP THE WITCHCRAFT THEM PLACE THIS BAG INSIDE THE BAG CONTAINING THE NEW INITIATES TORNED CUT CLOTHES FROM THE ROMPEMIENTO CEREMONY AND THE BODY OF THE ROOSTER. IT IS ONLY THOUGH THIS CEREMONY BY TAKING THE YAMBUZO TABLETS AND DRINKING THE OMIERO AND CHAMBA THAT AN INDIVIDUAL CAN TRUELY GET RID OF ANY WITCHCRAFT THAT HAS BEEN CAUSING THEM PAST OR PRESENT HARM.

STEP XIII

The Tata will then blow chamba and rum directly over the entire body of the new initiate and once again blow cigar smoke over the body and other areas that the individual will receive the Rayado "cuts". Using a new razor blade, the Tata will then cut some of the new initiates hair and wrap it in corn hush and wrap it using thread. This special package will be placed inside of the nganga of the spirit that the new initiate is making the pact with in exchange for the spirits protection. The belief and theory behind doing this is that if the spirit has something of you then they will know who you are by your unique smell. It is through smell that the spirits are able to locate us because spirits can't see as we do and can only see shadows like a blind man. The Tata then says to the initiate the following:

(**TATA**): *(Say the name of the new initiate), You have come here today seeking the protection of the spirits.*

(Say the name of the new initiate), May you always have a roof over your head. Sala Malekun, Malekun Sala.

May you always have food on your table. Sala Malekun, Malekun Sala.

(Say the name of the new initiate), May you always have money in your pockets. Sala Malekun, Malekun Sala.

(Say the name of the new initiate), May you always have good health. May you always have material possessions and wealth. Sala Malekun, Malekun Sala.

(Say the name of the new initiate), May you never be accused by your enemies.Sala Malekun, Malekun Sala.

(Say the name of the new initiate),May you never be arrested. Sala Malekun, Malekun Sala.

(Say the name of the new initiate), May you never be placed behind bars in jail. Sala Malekun, Malekun Sala.

(Say the name of the new initiate), May you never be in front of a judge against you. Sala Malekun, Malekun Sala.

(Say the name of the new initiate), May you always be victorious over all of your enemies known and unknown. Sala Malekun, Malekun Sala.

(Say the name of the new initiate),May the spirits always give you light in darkness. Sala Malekun, Malekun Sala.

(Say the name of the new initiate), May there never be any tragedy in your path. Sala Malekun, Malekun Sala.

(Say the name of the new initiate), May death never be in your path. Sala Malekun, Malekun Sala.

(Say the name of the new initiate), May illness never be in your path. Sala Malekun, Malekun Sala.

(Say the name of the new initiate), May you never be shot. Sala Malekun, Malekun Sala.

(Say the name of the new initiate), May you never be stabbed. Sala Malekun, Malekun Sala.

(Say the name of the new initiate), May you always avoid the spirit of death. Sala Malekun, Malekun Sala.

(Say the name of the new initiate), May the blood that spills today from your body be the only blood that every spells from your body. Sala Malekun, Malekun Sala.

(Say the name of the new initiate), May it be better that your blood spill here tonight in front of the Congo Spirits then it spill in the streets by some tragedy or some accident. Sala Malekun, Malekun Sala.

(Say the name of the new initiate), May this be the only blood that ever spills from your body. Sala Malekun, Malekun Sala.

(Say the name of the new initiate), May your blood give the spirits new life as they promise that they will give you new life. Sala Malekun, Malekun Sala.

(Say the name of the new initiate), May the spirits give you the ability like the deer to leap over your enemies. Sala Malekun, Malekun Sala.

(Say the name of the new initiate), May your enemies not see nor hear this ceremony here tonight. Sala Malekun, Malekun Sala.

STEP XIV

Using a new razor blade, the Tata will then proceed in doing the Rayado Initiation Ceremony by cutting the skin of the new initiate. As the Tata makes the cuts in the skin on the new initiate, the Bakunfula will rub the specially prepared powder called "*Polvo De Muerto*" directly into the cuts of the new initiate. As the Bakunfula or the Tata rubs the powder into the cuts of the new initiate, the wax from the white candle that was lighted at the beginning of the ceremony will be poured directly on top of the areas where the Rayado was done.

THE RAYADO SCRATCHINGS "CUTS" ARE DONE ON ALL OF THE FOLLOWING PLACES ON THE NEW INITIATES BODY: (BOTH SIDES OF THE UPPER TORSO, ON BOTH HANDS, ON BOTH SIDES OF THE BACK UPPER TORSO, ON THE BACK OF BOTH LEGS) THE RAYADO MARKS WILL BE ALWAYS CUT IN A SERIES OF (3) STRAIGHT LINES ON THE LEFT SIDE OF THE BODY. THE RAYADO MARKS WILL ALWAYS BE IN THE FORM OF A CROSS ON THE RIGHT SIDE OF THE BODY.

PLEASE SEE THE RAYADO DIAGRAM AT THE END OF THIS BOOK TO SEE THE ACTUAL AREAS IN WHICH AN INDIVIDUAL WILL RECEIVE THE RAYADO MARKS.

THIS IS THE CORRECT WAY TO RITUALLY GIVE AND TO PRESENT THE RAYADO MARKINGS. THE RAYADO MARKINGS "CUTS" SHOULD NOT BE MORE THAN 1 INCH IN LENGTH. IF THE RAYADO CEREMONY IS DONE CORRECTLY, THE MARKINGS WILL USUALLY HEAL BEFORE THE NEXT MORNING OR BEFORE 24 HOURS AFTER THE RITUAL RAYADO CEREMONY.

STEP XV

WHEN THE CUTS HAVE BEEN COMPLETELY SEALED WITH THE WHITE CANDLE WAX, THE TATA WILL SPIRITUALLY SEAL EACH OF THE RAYADO AREAS BY PRESSING THE MIRRORED END OF THE MPAKA AGAINST THE NEWLY CUT AREAS (STAMPING). AFTERWARDS, THE TATA WILL TELL THE NEW INITIATE TO OPEN THEIR MOUTH. WHEN THE NEW INITIATE OPENS THEIR MOUTH, THE CANDLE FLAME IS EXTINGUISHED DIRECTLY ON THE NEW INITIATE'S TONGUE.

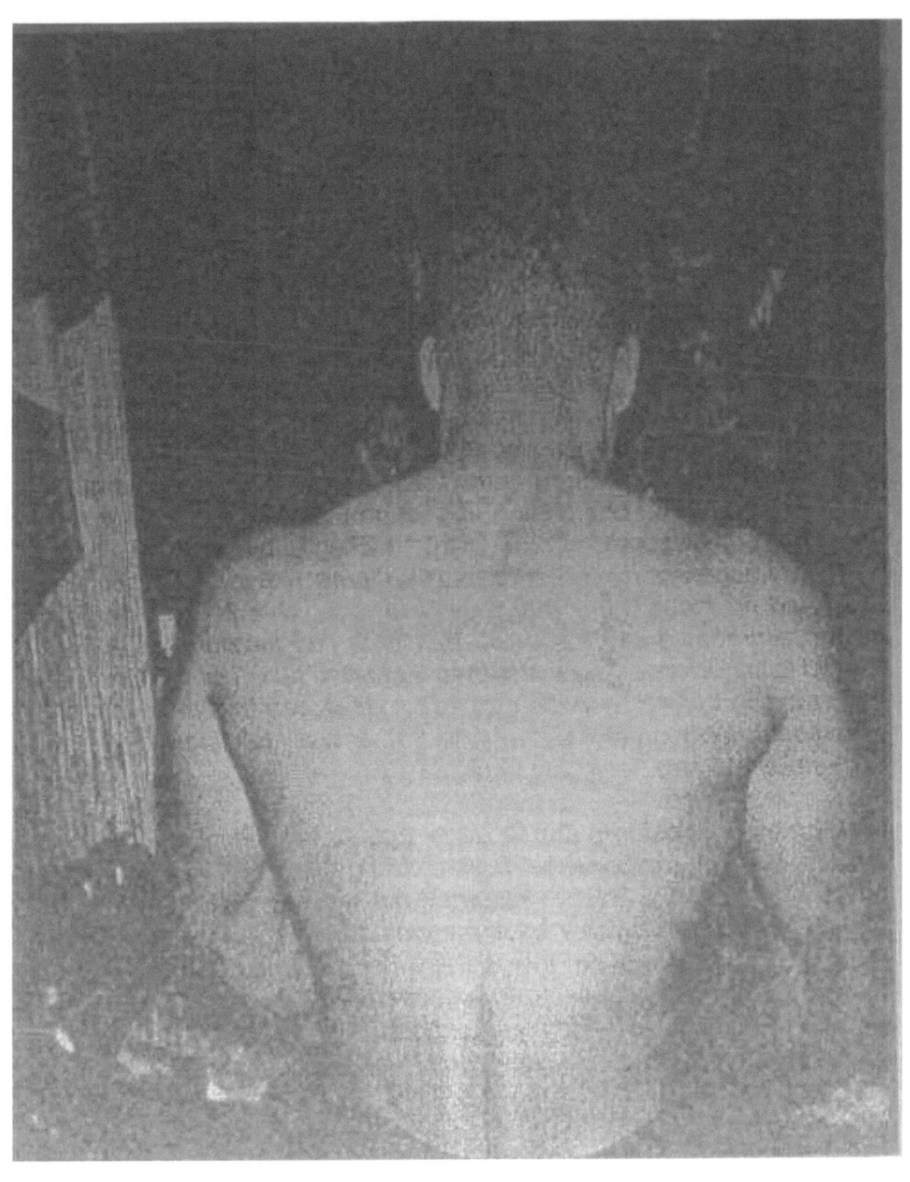

A new initiate receiving the Rayado Initiation Ceremony

STEP XVI

THE TATA OR THE BAKUNFULA WILL THEN CLEANSE THE NEW INITATE AGAIN WITH THE REMAINING LIVE ROOSTER ALONG WITH CLEANSING ALL OF THE OTHER MEMBERS THAT ARE THERE PRESENT. WHEN EVERY ONE HAS BEEN CLEANSED WITH THE ROOSTER, IT WILL THEN BE SACRIFICED AND THE BLOOD ALLOWED TO DRIP DIRECTLY INTO ONTO THE SPIRIT LUCERO AND THEN INTO THE NGANGA AND OVER THE SPIRIT BEADS THAT YOU WILL BE GIVING THE NEW INITIATE TO WEAR AFTER FEEDING THE CONGO SPIRITS.

HOW TO RITUALLY FEED THE SPIRITS

THE FOLLOWING IS HOW TO CORRECTLY SACRIFICE A ROOSTER/HEN DURING ANY CONGO RITUAL.

THE TATA WILL FIRST HAVE THE BAKUNFULA HOLDS THE ROOSTER TIGHTLY BY ITS LEGS AND ITS BODY. THE TATA WILL THEN SPRAY RUM OVER THE ROOSTER AND THEN BLOW CIGAR SMOKE OVER IT TO SANCTIFY THE SPIRIT OF THE ROOSTER. THE TATA WILL THEN PLACE THE MBELE TO THE NECK OF THE ROOSTER AND THEN SAY THE FOLLOWING BEFORE RITUALLY SLITTING THE THROAT OF THE ROOSTER TO FEED TO THE CONGO SPIRITS.

(**TATA**): (WHILE POINTING THE KNIFE AT THE THROAT OF THE ROOSTER BEFORE RITUALLY SACRIFICING IT TO THE CONGO SPIRITS WILL SAY:

(**TATA**): *"PUNTA"*

(**TATA & CONGO MEMBERS**): *MENGA*
THE TATA THEN SLITS THE THROAT OF THE BIRD AND AS THE BLOOD STARTS TO DRIP OUT THE FOLLOWING IS THEN SAID:

(TATA): *MENGA QUE VA A CORRER*

(**TATA & CONGO MEMBERS**): *COMO CORRE, COMO CORRE*

(TATA): *MENGA QUE VA A CORRER*

(TATA & CONGO MEMBERS): *COMO CORRE, COMO CORRE*

(TATA): *MENGA QUE VA A CORRER*

(TATA & CONGO MEMBERS): *COMO CORRE, COMO CORRE*

(TATA): MBELE ESTA COMIENDO

(TATA & CONGO MEMBERS): *COMO CORRE, COMO CORRE*

(TATA): MBELE ESTA COMIENDO

(TATA & CONGO MEMBERS): *COMO CORRE, COMO CORRE*

(TATA): LUCERITO ESTA COMIENDO

(TATA & CONGO MEMBERS): *COMO CORRE, COMO CORRE*

(TATA): LUCERITO ESTA COMIENDO

(TATA & CONGO MEMBERS): *COMO CORRE, COMO CORRE*

(TATA): (SAY THE NAME OF THE SPIRIT NGANGA) *ESTA COMIENDO*

(TATA & CONGO MEMBERS): *COMO CORRE, COMO CORRE*

(TATA): (SAY THE NAME OF THE SPIRIT NGANGA) *ESTA COMIENDO*

(TATA & CONGO MEMBERS): *COMO CORRE, COMO CORRE*

(TATA): *LUCERITO ESTA COMIENDO*

(TATA & CONGO MEMBERS): *COMO CORRE, COMO CORRE*

(TATA): *MENGA QUE VA A CORRER*

(TATA & CONGO MEMBERS): *COMO CORRE, COMO CORRE*

(TATA): *MENGA QUE VA A CORRER*

(TATA & CONGO MEMBERS): *COMO CORRE, COMO CORRE*

THE TATA WILL THEN WASH THE MBELE WITH THE WHITE RUM AND ALLOW IT TO DRIP CLEAN INTO THE NGANGA. AFTER THIS THE TATA WILL THEN SPRAY RUM AND BLOW CIGAR SMOKE ONTO THE SPIRIT LUCERO AND INTO THE SPIRIT NGANGA.

STEP XVII

The Tata and the Bakunfula will then take the Human Skull *(KIYUMBA)* from the nganga, a glass of water and a white candle and hold it in front face of the new initiate. The lighted white candle will be held behind the glass of fresh water with a crucifix inside and behind these items the *Kiyumba* (skull) As the blind fold is removed from the new initiate the Tata will say to the individual the following:

(TATA): *Tell me what do you see?*

(NEW INITIATE): The new initiate will respond with what they think they see.

(TATA): *The Crucifix in the water represents Nzambi (GOD) and the water around it represents protection, purity and a cleansed spiritual path, the candle represents the protective light that the spirits will give you in the world of darkness and the skull represents the Congo Spirits that you have made a pact with through this sacred initiation.*

(TATA): *May the Congo Spirits which give you light also give you new life and all the good things that life and destiny holds for you.*

STEP XVIII

The new initiate is made to lay face down on the floor directly in front of the nganga. When they are lying face down, each member will use the sacred ritual MBELE *"machete"* and hit the new initiate with the flat side of the machete (21) times each. The new initiate will then be told that if every they disobey the "*CONGO SPIRITS"*, the "*TATA"*,the "*BAKUNFULA"*, the other "*TEMPLEMEMBERS"*, or the "*REGLAS DE CONGO*" of their Congo Munanzo that they are being initiated into that they will be punished in this same manner in front of the spirits by the TATA and or by the BAKUNFULA.

WHEN AN INDIVIDUAL BECOMES A MEMBER OF A CONGO MUNANZO THEY AGREE TO BE PUNISHED AND DISCIPLINED IN FRONT OF THE CONGO SPIRITS BY THE TATA OR THE BAKUNFULA FOR BREAKING OR VIOLATING ANY OF THE SACRED OATHS, RULES & REGULATIONS OF THE CONGO MUNANZO.

IF YOU ARE AN INDIVIDUAL WHO DOES NOT LIKE TO LISTEN OR OBEY RULES THEN THE FORMAL CONGO MUNANZO IS NOT FOR YOU. YOU BETTER THINK IT OVER BEFORE YOU GET INITIATED.

STEP XIX

The new initiate is then lifted off the floor by the Tata and the Bakunfula and shown how to salute the Tata and the other members of the Congo Temple. This special salute is done each and every time you see your Tata or any other member from your Congo temple.

THIS VERY UNIQUE SALUTE WHICH INCLUDES A SECRET HAND SHAKE MAY VARY FROM TEMPLE TO TEMPLE. THE SECRET HAND SHAKE IS HOW YOU WILL BE ABLE TO IDENTIFY OTHER INDIVIDUALS WHO HAVE BEEN INIITIATED INTO THE CONGO MYSTERIES FROM YOUR PARTICULAR CONGO TEMPLE.

STEP XX

The new initiate will then go with the other members from the Congo Munanzo and dispose of the bag of items containing the dead roosters, the new initiate's cut/torn cloths and whatever else that the Congo spirits instruct the members to place in the bag.

After disposing of the bag, the new initiate will return to the Congo Munanzo where they will sleep in front of the nganga the entire night on a straw mat.

After the new initiate wakes up in the morning they will once again take a bath by themselves using the same omiero herbal mixture that they used for the Rayado initiation. This bath should be taken by the initiate at their respected homes for three consecutive days.

Most Congo temples require all new initiates to sleep in front of the nganga for three consecutive nights so that the spirits can begin to know and to assist the new initiate to resolve any problems that they may have in their path. By sleeping in front of the nganga which gave birth to your Rayado initiation you will start to be able to see, hear, and to smell the spirits. The Rayado ceremony opens up the third eye of an individual and therefore you will want to spend as much time with the Congo Spirits as possible in order to develop and fine tune your new psychic spiritual and magical abilities.

IF YOU HAVE BEEN INITIATED INTO THE CONGO MYSTERIES AND DID NOT SPEND THE NIGHT IN FRONT OF THE NGANGA OF YOUR CONGO MUNANZO YOU DID NOT HAVE THE CEREMONY DONE CORRECTLY.

IN MOST CONGO MUNANZOS, FOLLOWING THE RAYADO CEREMONY THE NEW INITIATE IS GIVEN A HEAD ROGATION CLEANSING "ROGACION DE LA CABEZA" TO FURTHER SPIRITUALLY STRENGTHEN THE NEW INITIATES RELATIONSHIP WITH THE POWERFUL CONGO SPIRITS TO OPEN UP AND TO DEVELOP THE NEW INITIATE'S THIRD EYE. A HEAD ROGATION WILL STABLIZE THE NEW INITIATE'S PERSONAL SPIRIT GUIDES.

THE SECOND RAYADO INITIATION RITUAL

THE SECOND RAYADO SHOULD TAKE PLACE (21) DAYS AFTER THE FIRST RAYADO. THE INITIATION PROCESS IS THE SAME FOR THE SECOND RAYADO PROCESS EXCEPT FOR THE FOLLOWING:

(1) *THE INDIVIDUAL NO LONGER HAS TO WEAR A BLIND FOLD.*

(2) *THE INDIVIDUAL IS NOT HIT WITH THE MACHETE BY THE MEMBERS OF THE TEMPLE.*

(3) *THE MARKS OF THE SECOND RAYADO RITUAL ARE DONE DIRECTLY ON TOP AND IN THE SAME PLACE AS THE FIRST ONES ON THE NEW INITIATES BODY.*

(4) *AFTER RECEIVING THE SECOND RAYADO, THE NEW INITIATE IS GIVEN A SPECIAL SET OF SPIRIT BEADS CALLED "COLLAR DE MUERTO" THE COLLAR DE MUERTO IS ALSO KNOWN AS THE "COLLAR DE LA BANDERA". THIS POWERFUL COLLAR IS A LONG STRAND OF BEADS THAT CONTAINS VARIOUS COLOR PATTERNS OF EACH OF THE CONGO SPIRITS, A SMALL CHAIN AND A COWRIE SHELL THAT IS PREPARED, PACKED AND SEALED WITH POWERFUL MAGICAL INGREDIENTS THAT WILL PROTECT THE INDIVIDUAL AND GIVE THEM SPECIAL MAGICAL ABILITIES. THE COLLAR DE MUERTO IS WORN OVER THE SHOULDRERS AND ACCROSS THE CHEST (LEFT SHOULDER TO RIGHT SIDE WAIST) AT CEREMONIES.*

IF THE COWRIE SHELL ON THE COLLAR DE MUERTO HAS NOT BEEN FILLED UP WITH THE SECRET MAGICAL INGREDIENTS BY THE TATA AND THEN SEALED, THE CEREMONY WAS NOT DONE CORRECTLY.

The traditional Congo Spirit Nganga of the Congo Spirit Zarabanda

HOW TO MAKE THE SACRED SPIRIT OMIERO

The number of fresh herbs used in the preparation of the omiero depends on the particular spirit being invokes and prepared. The following is a chart for the number of herbs attributed to each of the major Congo Spirit deities.

GENERAL OMIERO *- 21 OR 121 HERBS*

LUCERO OMIERO *- 21 OR 121 HERBS*

EGGUN OMIERO *- 9, 21 OR 121 HERBS*

CENTELLE NDOKI OMIERO *- 9 HERBS*

ZARABANDA OMIERO *- 9 HERBS*

TIEMBLA TIERRA OMIERO *- 8 HERBS*

MADRE DE AGUA OMIERO *- 7 HERBS*

MAMA SHOLAN OMIERO *- 5 HERBS*

CABO RONDO OMIERO *- 7 HERBS*

PRENDA JUDIA OMIERO - 9, *21, 121 HERBS*

OZAIN OMIERO *- 21 OR 121 HERBS*

BRAZO FUERTE OMIERO *- 6 HERBS*

SIETE RAYOS OMIERO *- 6 or 7 HERBS*

KOBAYENDE OMIERO *- 16 HERBS*

NSAMBA NTALA OMIERO *- 2, 4 OR 21 HERBS*

AJE SPIRITS OMIERO *- 9, 21 OR 121 HERBS*

ITEMS NECESSARY TO PREPARE THE OMIERO

1. ONE LARGE BOWL
2. TWENTY-ONE GRAINS OF PARADISE
3. BEE'S HONEY
4. POWDERED SMOKED FISH
5. POWDERED SMOKED JUTIA
6. CIGARS
7. RUM
8. (4) PIECES OF PREPARED COCONUTS FOR DIVINATION
9. ONE STRAW MAT (ESTERA)
10. PEMBA
11. FRESH HERBS
12. FRESH WATER
13. HOLY WATER
14. MAY RAIN WATER
15. COCONUT WATER

(HOLY WATER FROM A CHURCH IS OPTIONAL)

PREPARATION

1. Lay the straw mat on the floor.

2. Place the large bowl which you will be preparing the Omiero into the center of the straw mat.

3. Pour all of the waters into the bowl.

4. Place all of the herbs on the mat.

5. Spray the herbs with rum and blow the smoke from a cigar over all of the herbs.

6. Place all of the items which you will be using to prepare the omiero on the mat.

7. Light a white candle and place it next to the bowl.

8. Pick up all of the herbs in both of your hands and hold them up to the sky and say and do the following:

CON LA BENDICION Y LA LICENCIA DE NSAMBI -

SALA MALEKUN, MALEKUN SALA

CON LA BENDICION Y LA LICENCIA DE EGGUN -

SALA MALEKUN, MALEKUN SALA

CON LA BENDICION Y LA LICENCIA DE LUCERO - SALA MALEKUN, MALEKUN SALA

CON LA BENDICION Y LA LICENCIA DE OZAIN - SALA MALEKUN, MALEKUN SALA

CON LA BENDICION Y LA LICENCIA DE - SAY THE NAME OF THE SPIRIT - SALA MALEKUN, MALEKUN SALA

9. After saying the above prayer, kiss the herbs in your hands three times and then begin to pull off all of the leaves and place them into the bowl.

10. Sitting in a chair in front of the bowl, begin ripping and tearing the herbs in the waters. This is called making *"Ozain."*

11. Sing the following mambo while making the omiero:

MA MA MA IYA IYA IYA.
MA MA MA IYA IYA IYA.
MA MA MA IYA IYA IYA.
EBO EBO EBO EBO EBO
EBO EBO EBO EBO EBO
EWE EWE EWE EWE EWE
EWE EWE EWE EWE EWE
MA MA MA IYA IYA IYA.
MA MA MA IYA IYA IYA.
MA MA MA IYA IYA IYA.
EBO EBO EBO EBO EBO
EBO EBO EBO EBO EBO
EWE EWE EWE EWE EWE
EWE EWE EWE EWE EWE

REPEAT THIS SONG UNTIL YOU HAVE FINISHED PREPARING THE OMIERO.

12. When you have finished, add the following items into the omiero liquid; honey, grains of paradise, smoked fish and jutia.

13. Check with the four coconut pieces in the divination ritual to see if the omiero has been prepared correctly.

14. If the answer comes with a yes then drip candle wax into the omiero liquid. The amount of drops will depend on the spirit omiero being prepared. Use the chart on the first page of this chapter. (For example if the omiero is for the Spirit Zarabanda then place 9 drops of candle wax into the omiero)

THE CANDLE WAX SEALS THE MAGICAL POWER (ACHE) OF HERBS INTO THE SACRED OMIERO -

HOW TO PREPARE THE SACRED RAYADO POWDER

The Following sacred formula is one version about how to correctly prepare the sacred *Rayado Initiation Powder.* This sacred powder may be prepared in a different manner depending on the Congo religious system which are being initiated into. If you received your *Rayado Initiation Ceremony* and the Tata did not place this sacred *Rayado Initiation Powder* into the Rayado *"scratchings"* your Rayado was not done correctly. It is only by placing this sacred powder into your Rayado *"scratchings"* that the new initiate will be spiritually connected to the Congo Spirits. If you did not have this done during your *Rayado Initiation Ceremony* the Congo Spirits will not be able to protect you nor will they be able to recognize you as one of their own children. This sacred powder is also referred to as *"Polvo De Muerto"* by the initiates of Caribbean Palo Mayombe religious tradition.

*IF THE RAYADO POWDER IS **"NOT"** PREPARED CORRECTLY AND IT IS PLACED INTO THE RAYADO "SCRATCHINGS" OF THE NEW INITIATE IT WILL BE ALMOST IMPOSSIBLE TO REMOVE IT FROM THEIR BODIES. THIS CAN BE EXTREMELY SPIRITUALLY DAMAGING TO THE SPIRITUAL WELL BEING OF THE NEW INITIATE. IF THE RAYADO POWDER IS NOT PREPARED CORRECTLY THE NEW INITIATE CAN DEVELOP TERMINAL ILLNESS AND CAUSE THE EVENTUAL DEATH OF THE NEW INITIATE.*

THIS IS ANOTHER ONE OF THOSE TRAGIC STORIES THAT I HAVE SEEN AND HEARD HAPPENING TO 1000's OF INNOCENT INDIVIDUALS DESIRING TO RECEIVE THE AUTHENTIC MYSTERIES OF THE CONGO RELIGION. IN MANY OF THESE TRAGIC STORIES THAT THE NEW INITIATE WAS "SCRATCHED INTO PALO", THE TATA ONLYUSED THE ASH FROM A CIGAR OR ABSOLUTELY NOTHING AT ALL TO PACK THE"SCRATCHES" WITH. THIS IS NOT THE CORRECT

WAY TO RECEIVE THE RAYADO INITIATION CEREMONY. IF YOU HAVE ALREADY RECEIVED YOUR RAYADO INITIATION AND THERE WAS NOTHING PACKED INTO THE "SCRATCHINGS" OR IF THEY ONLY USED THE ASH FROM A CIGAR, YOU GOT "RIPPED OFF."

MAKE SURE THAT THE CONGO MUNANZO THAT YOU ARE GETTING INITIATED INTO IS LEGITIMATE AND THAT THE TATA REALLY KNOWS WHAT HE IS DOING. "DON'T GET BURNED". AN INCORRECT RAYADO INITIATION CEREMONY IS A DISASTER JUST WAITING TO HAPPEN TO THE NEW INITIATE.

INGREDIENTS NECESSARY

DIRT FROM 121 TOMBS
DIRT FROM 121 DIFFERENT LOCATIONS
HUMAN BONE POWDER
121 POWDERED HERBS
121 POWDERED PALOS
DEER HORN POWDER
POWDERED ACHE DE SANTO HERB (OPTIONAL)

THIS IS THE AUTHENTIC "ORIGINAL" BASIC RAYADO INITIATION POWDER FORMULA ALTHOUGH THERE MAY BE OTHER SACRED RELIGIOUS INGREDIENTS ADDED TO IT DEPENDING ON THE MYSTERIES OF THE PARTICULAR CONGO MUNANZO THAT YOU ARE GETTING INITIATED INTO.

IF THE TATA FROM YOUR MUNANZO TELLS YOU THAT IN THEIR CONGO RELIGIOUS TRADITION THAT THEY ONLY USE *"CIGAR ASH"* OR *"NOTHING"*AT ALL IN THE RAYADO INITIATION CEREMONY YOU HAVE BEEN "RIPPED OFF" AND THAT INDIVIDUAL DOESN'T KNOW WHAT THEY ARE DOING. IF THIS IS THE CASE THEN YOU SHOULD FIND A QUALIFIED TATA TO FIX IT RIGHT AWAY.

HOW TO PREPARE THE YAMBUZO FOR THE RAYADO

The sacred *Yambuzo Tablets* are made of the same ingredients as the *Rayado Initiation Powder* but are formed into tablets or spiritual pills using bee's honey to make and to form them. When a new initiate is given these very powerful magical ingredients to swallow, if the individual has any witchcraft or negative energy within their bodies these sacred ingredients will cause them to vomit it up and thus removing it from their bodies making the individual spiritually clean. The new initiate is given (3) *Yambuzo Tablets* to swallow along with the sacred ritual *Congo Spirit Omiero* to drink.

IF YOU RECEIVED YOUR RAYADO INITIATION CEREMONY AND YOU WERE NOT GIVEN YAMBUZO TABLETS TO SWALLOW, THEN YOUR RAYADO WAS NOT DONE CORRECTLY. THESE SACRED INGREDIENTS ARE KEY ELEMENTS TO SPIRITUALLY PREPARING THE BODY OF THE NEW INITIATE TO BE ABLE TO WORK WITH THE CONGO SPIRITS.

THIS VERY IMPORTANT ASPECT OF THE RAYADO INITIATION CEREMONY IS COMMON TO ALL CONGO RELIGIOUS MAGICAL BELIEFS NO MATTER WHAT RELIGIOUS TRADITION THAT YOU COME FROM.

IF YOU WERE NOT GIVEN THE SACRED YAMBUZO TABLETS TO SWALLOW YOUR RAYADO INITIATION CEREMONY WAS NOT DONE CORRECTLY.

INGREDIENTS NECESSARY

DIRT FROM 121 TOMBS
DIRT FROM 121 DIFFERENT LOCATIONS
HUMAN BONE POWDER
121 POWDERED HERBS
121 POWDERED PALOS
POWDERED ACHE DE SANTO HERB (OPTIONAL)
DEER HORN POWDER
BEE'S HONEY

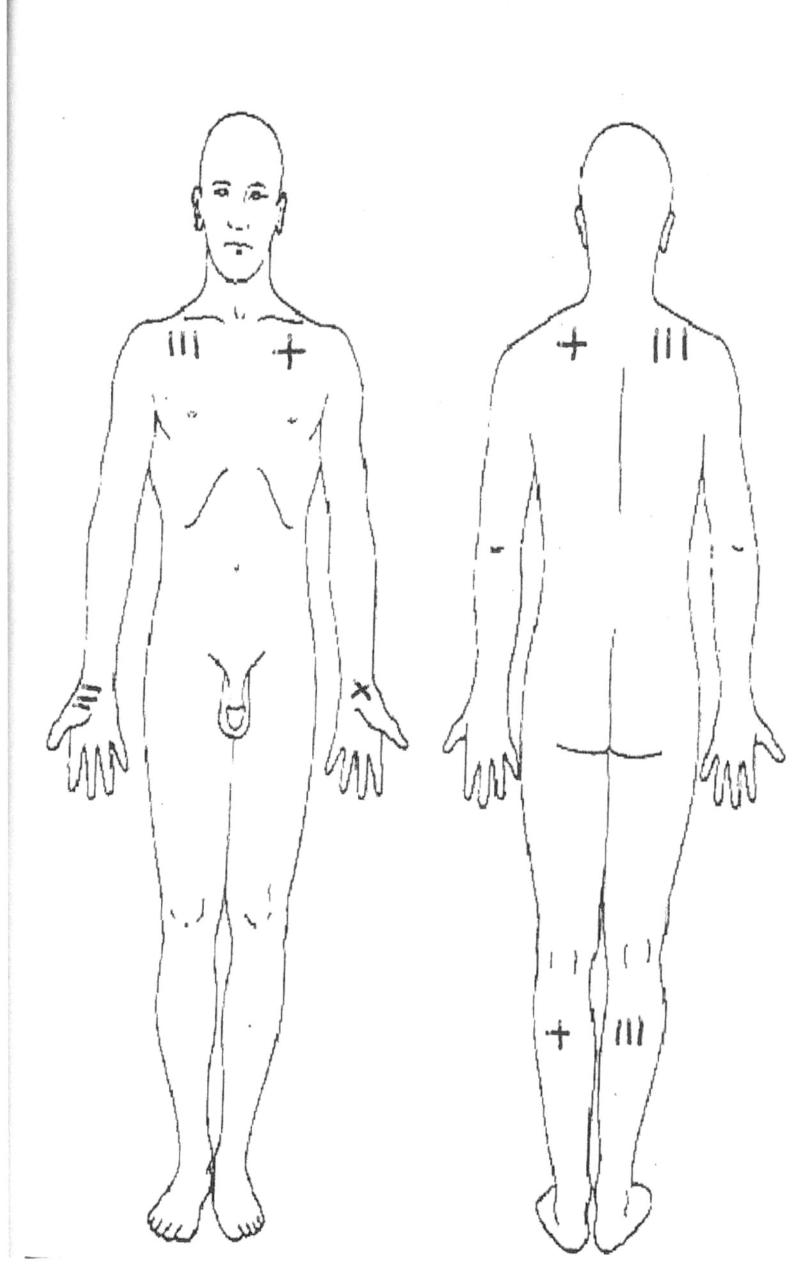

A DIAGRAM SHOWING THE RAYADO MARKS (MAN)

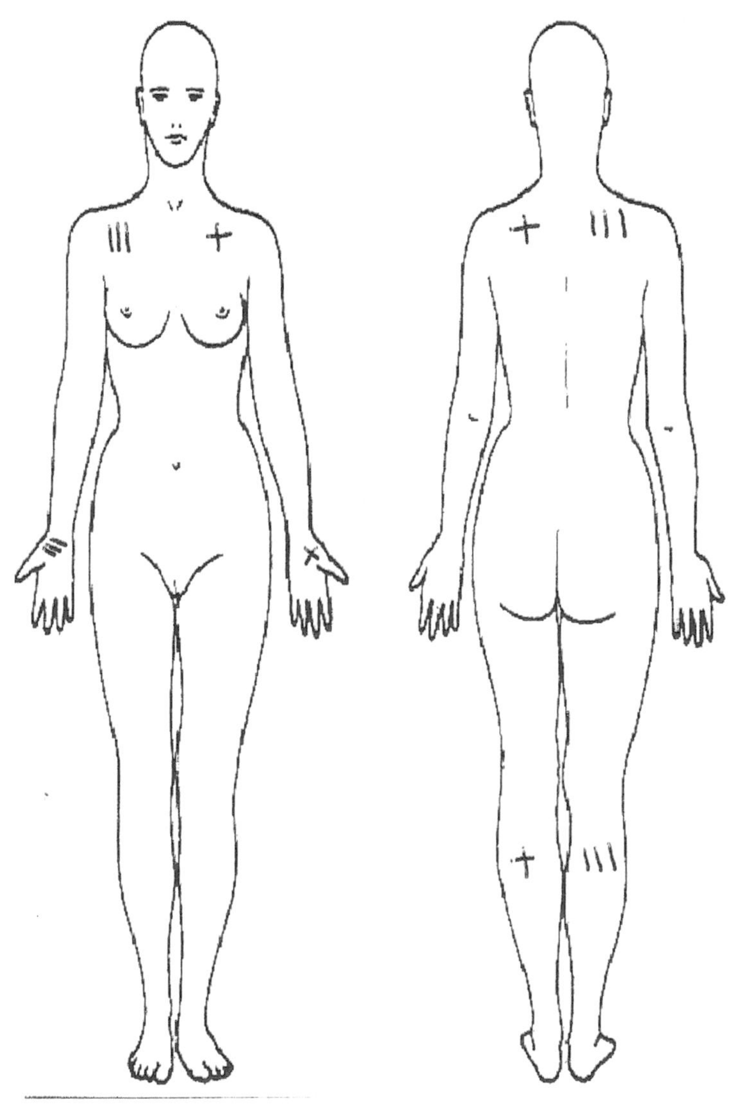

A DIAGRAM SHOWING THE RAYADO MARKS (WOMAN)

PAPA MONTENEGRO'S OCCULT SHOP

PAPA MONTENEGRO'S OCCULT SHOP would like to invite you to browse through our store and shop with confidence.

Authentic Handmade Occult Products, Quimbanda Ritual Products, Herbal Baths, Colognes, Incense, Oils, Powders, Spell Kits, Candles, Books & Sacred Art. All of our occult products are handmade.

WE CARRY OVER 400 AUTHENTIC HANDMADE & RITUALLY PREPARED OCCULT OILS IN STOCK AT OUR STORE, MADE WITH REAL MAGICAL HERBS, ESSENTIAL OILS, FRAGRANCED OILS & RARE OCCULT SACRED INGREDIENTS.

WWW.PAPAMONTENEGRO.COM

www.ingramcontent.com/pod-product-compliance
Ingram Content Group UK Ltd.
Pitfield, Milton Keynes, MK11 3LW, UK
UKHW041923190726
13854UKWH00003B/1406

9 781105 750939